A.P.J. ABDUL KALAM

RAMESWARAM...A TINY ISLAND OFF THE COAST OF THE SOUTHERN STATE OF TAMIL NADU, WITH ONLY THE PAMBAN BRIDGE TO CONNECT IT TO THE MAINLAND.

SO REMOTE IT WAS IN THE EARLY 1900s, IT IS HARD TO IMAGINE THAT A LITTLE BOY FROM THAT FAR CORNER WOULD ONE DAY BECOME A MAN WHO EARNED A TRULY SPECIAL PLACE IN THE HEARTS OF HIS COUNTRYMEN.

*JALAL USED TO CALL HIM AZAD. POSSIBLY A REFERENCE TO HIS NAMESAKE, THE FREEDOM FIGHTER ABUL KALAM AZAD.

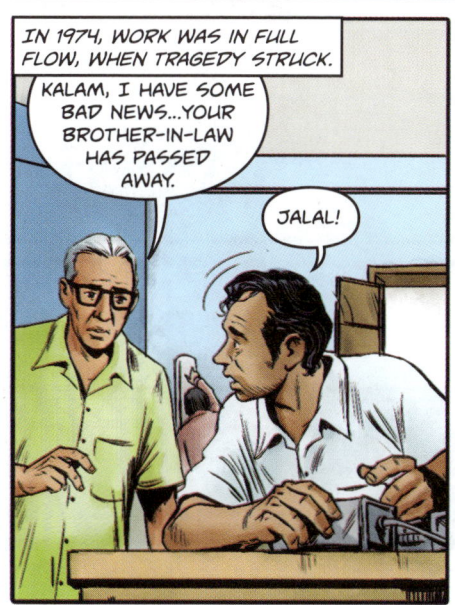

"A BOY WHO KNEW THAT NO MATTER WHAT, THERE WAS ALWAYS A PAIR OF LOVING HANDS TO HOLD...THOSE HANDS GONE FOREVER. OH JALAL, I AM ALL ALONE NOW!"

ZOHRA WAS INCONSOLABLE.

SOB! SOB! SOB!

"I CANNOT DO THIS, SIR... NOTHING MAKES SENSE ANYMORE. EVERYTHING SEEMS SO FUTILE."

"YOU HAVE SUFFERED A VERY BIG LOSS BUT YOUR WORK WILL GIVE YOU SOLACE."

IN THE NEXT TWO YEARS, ABDUL'S FATHER AND THEN HIS MOTHER PASSED AWAY. AS HE SAT IN THE MOSQUE OF HIS CHILDHOOD, MOURNING THEIR LOSS –

"They carried out the task I designed for them, with dedication and honesty and then came back to me. Why are you mourning their day of accomplishment? Concentrate on your work and proclaim my glory through your deeds."

NOBODY HAD SPOKEN THESE WORDS, BUT ABDUL HEARD THEM LOUD AND CLEAR. THE NEXT MORNING HE RETURNED TO THUMBA AND THREW HIMSELF INTO HIS WORK.

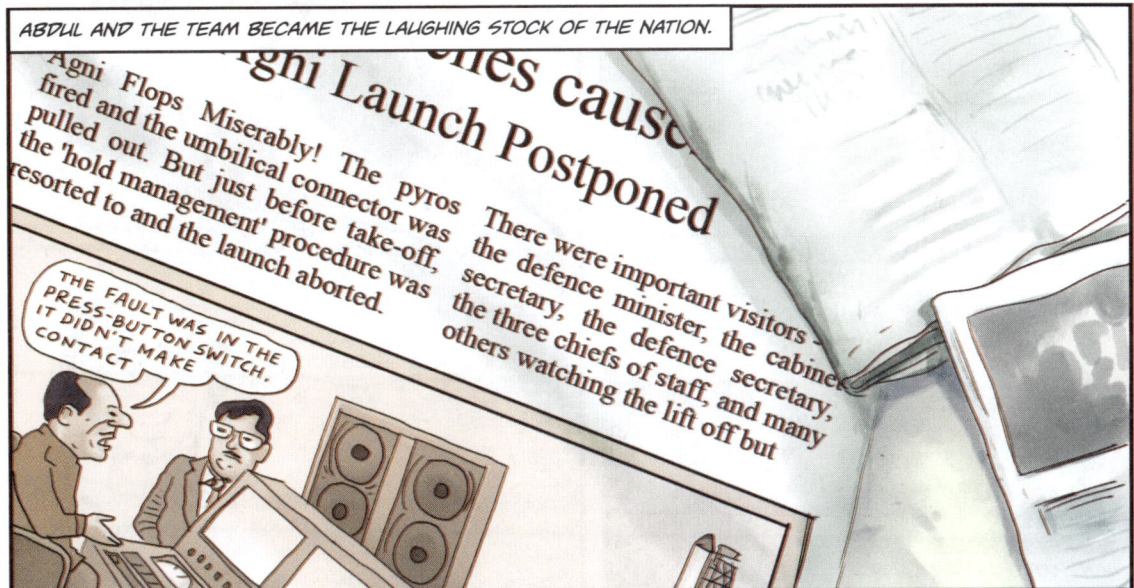

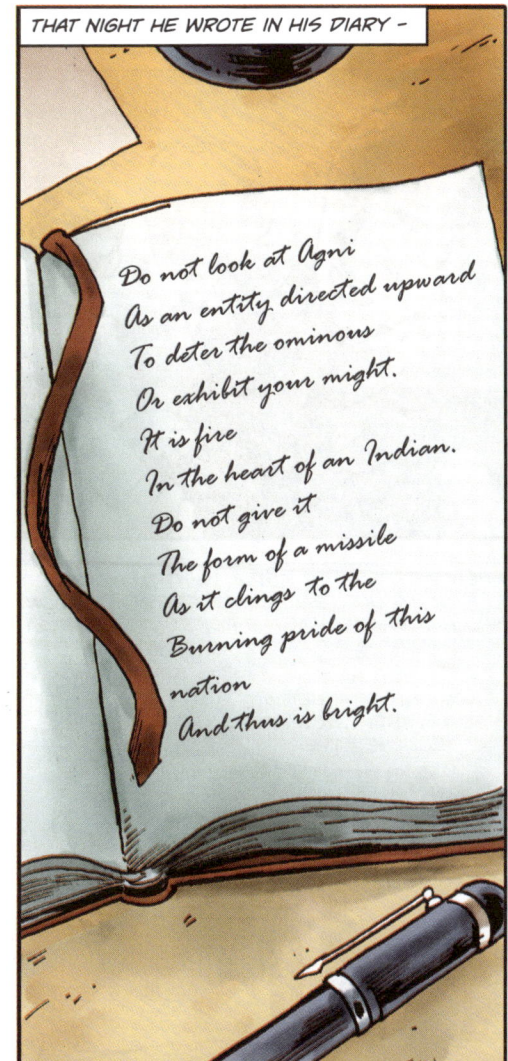

*TAKEN FORWARD

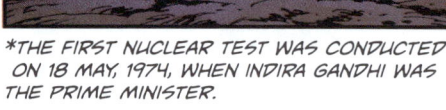

*NAMED AFTER THE RIVERS BRAHMAPUTRA IN INDIA AND MOSKVA IN RUSSIA

*A SMALL AIRCRAFT

AND SO WAS BORN THE IDEA OF HAVING P.U.R.A. VILLAGE CLUSTERS – INSTITUTIONS, HOSPITALS AND EMPLOYMENT OPPORTUNITIES SPREAD ACROSS A GROUP OF VILLAGES WELL CONNECTED BY ROAD – SO THAT LIFE IN THE VILLAGES WOULD BE PROSPEROUS AND HEALTHY.

ABDUL WAS SO HAPPY WITH THIS THOUGHT THAT HE DONATED HIS LIFE'S SAVINGS TO THE PROJECT.

BY NOW, PEOPLE HAD REALISED THAT THEIR 'MISSILE MAN' WAS ALSO A VERY CARING PERSON. EVERYWHERE HE WENT, HE WAS GREETED BY HORDES OF INDIANS WHO SOMETIMES WAITED ALL DAY TO GET A GLIMPSE OF HIM.

FOR THE YOUNG, HE HAD BECOME AN ICON, A MENTOR AND THE GO-TO PERSON WHEN THEY WERE IN TROUBLE OR DOUBT.

Dear Kalam Uncle, I was good in studies but now I feel so much stress that I could not get into medical college....

FOREIGN MEDIA COMMENTED ON HIS 'ROCKSTAR' LIKE BUZZ AND HE WAS EVEN NOMINATED TWICE FOR MTV'S YOUTH ICON OF THE YEAR AWARD. IT DID NOT MATTER THAT HE WAS THEN MORE THAN 73 YEARS OLD!

ABDUL TURNED OUT TO BE POPULAR AND EFFECTIVE EVEN IN HIS STATE VISITS TO OTHER COUNTRIES.

IN SWITZERLAND –

SWITZERLAND WILL CELEBRATE 26 MAY AS SCIENCE DAY, TO COMMEMORATE DR KALAM'S VISIT.

IN SOUTH AFRICA –

I GIVE TO YOU THE PAN AFRICAN E-NETWORK THAT WILL CONNECT INDIA AND THE 53-MEMBER NATIONS OF THIS GREAT CONTINENT TO EACH OTHER, AND PROVIDE EDUCATION, HEALTHCARE AND E-GOVERNANCE SERVICES.

AS PRESIDENT, ABDUL WAS ALSO THE SUPREME COMMANDER OF THE ARMED FORCES. HE MADE IT A POINT TO VISIT HIS MEN POSTED IN DIFFICULT TERRAINS. HE VISITED THE KUMAR POST ON SIACHEN GLACIER AND RODE IN THE NAVAL SUBMARINE, INS SINDHURAKSHAK.

BUT HIS MOST CHERISHED MOMENT CAME IN JUNE 2006, WHEN HE VISITED AN AIR FORCE BASE IN PUNE.

THE MISSION COMPUTERS AND OTHER EQUIPMENT OF THIS SUKHOI HAVE ALL BEEN MADE IN INDIA.

VERY GOOD. THAT IS HOW IT SHOULD BE.

YOU KNOW, I ONCE DREAMED OF BECOMING A FIGHTER PILOT LIKE YOU. IT WAS MY BIGGEST DREAM.

I COULD TRAIN YOU, SIR. YOU COULD FLY WITH ME AS A CO-PILOT.

NEVER ONE TO REFUSE A CHALLENGE, ABDUL UNDERTOOK THE TRAINING AND THE NEXT DAY...

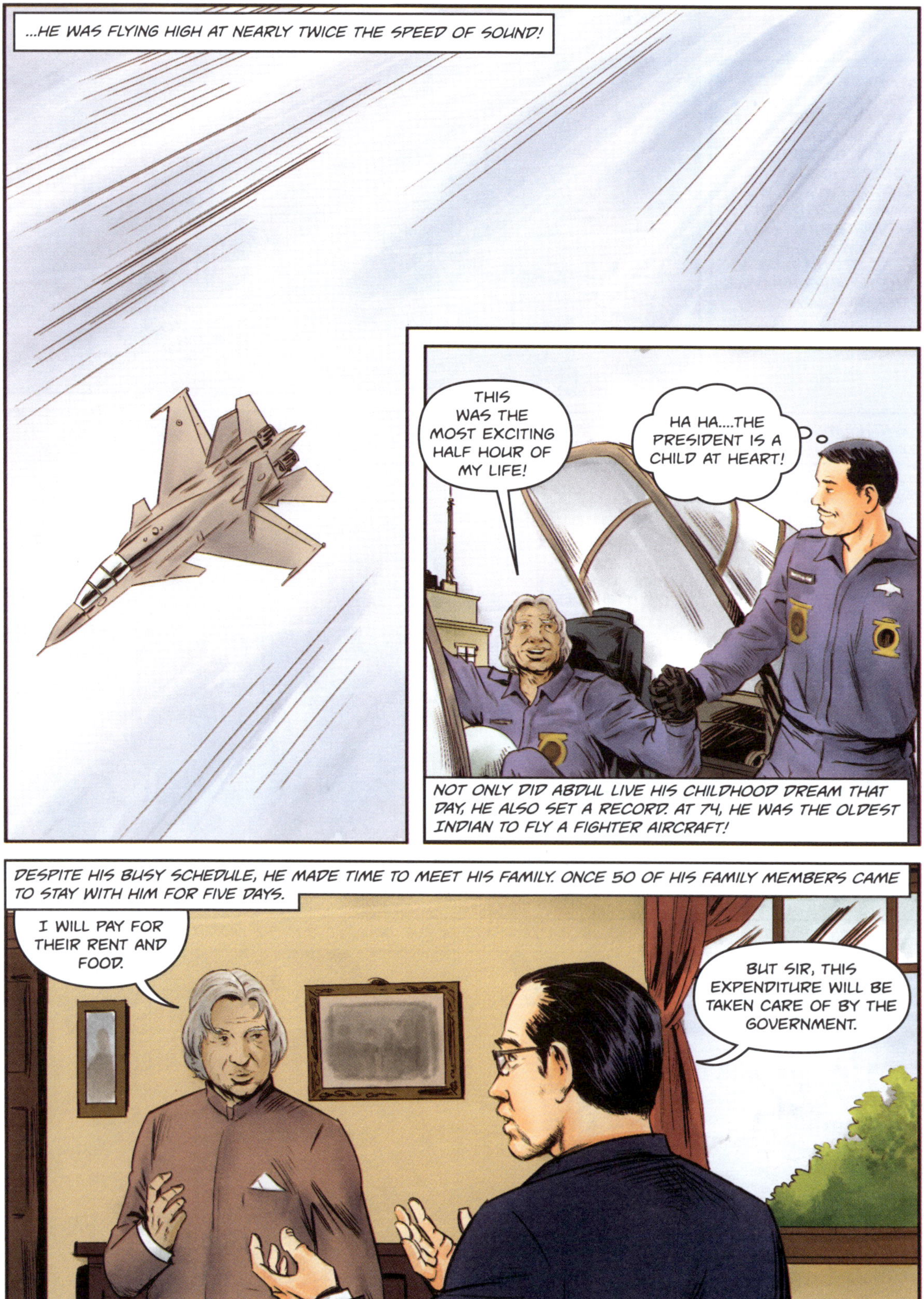

THE PUBLIC OUTPOURING OF GRIEF THAT FOLLOWED WAS UNPRECEDENTED. FROM SHILLONG, TO DELHI AND TO RAMESWARAM HIS FINAL RESTING PLACE, THE MASSES THRONGED THE STREETS TO PAY THEIR RESPECTS TO THE 'PEOPLE'S PRESIDENT'. A PROUD AND PRACTISING MUSLIM BUT EQUALLY RESPECTFUL OF ALL OTHER RELIGIONS, A STOREHOUSE OF KNOWLEDGE BUT AN ETERNAL LEARNER, A HUMANITARIAN AND A TRUE INDIAN.

OBITUARIES CAME IN FROM ALL CORNERS OF THE WORLD FOR HE HAD TOUCHED MANY LIVES, BUT WHAT ABDUL ONCE SAID ABOUT HIMSELF IS PERHAPS WHAT DESCRIBES HIM BEST –

"I am a well in this great land
Looking at its million boys and girls
To draw from me
The inexhaustible divinity
And spread His grace everywhere
As does the water drawn from a well."

He often said, "my dream is to see a billion smiles on billion faces"

There was no place for hierarchies and ranks in his life.

He was India's greatest President and will be so for a long time

Dr. Kalam radiated positive energy

If a country is to be corruption free and become a nation of beautiful minds, I strongly feel there are three key societal members who can make a difference. They are the father, the mother and the teacher.

— A.P.J. Abdul Kalam